# Celebrating Rosh Hashanah

Katie Peters

GRL Consultant Diane Craig,
Certified Literacy Specialist

Lerner Publications ◆ Minneapolis

**Note from a GRL Consultant**
This Pull Ahead leveled book has been carefully designed for beginning readers. A team of guided reading literacy experts has reviewed and leveled the book to ensure readers pull ahead and experience success.



Lerner Publications
An imprint of Lerner Publishing Group, Inc.
241 First Avenue North
Minneapolis, MN 55401 USA

For reading levels and more information, look up this title at www.lernerbooks.com.

Main body text set in Memphis Pro 24/39
Typeface provided by Linotype.

Photo Acknowledgments
The images in this book are used with the permission of: © Kovaleva_Ka/Shutterstock Images, p. 3; © SeventyFour/Shutterstock Images, pp. 4–5; © Drazen/Adobe Stock, pp. 6–7, 16 (left); © Gorodenkoff/Shutterstock Images, pp. 8–9; © Finist4/Shutterstock Images, pp. 10–11, 16 (middle); © Noam/Adobe Stock, pp. 12–13, 16 (right); © paparazzza/Shutterstock Images, pp. 14–15.

Front Cover: © Rimma Bondarenko/Shutterstock Images

**Library of Congress Cataloging-in-Publication Data**

Names: Peters, Katie, author.
Title: Celebrating Rosh Hashanah / written by Katie Peters.
Description: Minneapolis : Lerner Publications, [2026] | Series: Let's celebrate holidays (Pull ahead readers–nonfiction) | Includes index. | Audience: Ages 4–7 | Audience: Grades K–1 | Summary: "Rosh Hashanah is a day of new beginnings. Easy-to-read text and engaging photographs show readers how to celebrate the Jewish New Year. Pairs with the fiction title, Our Family Celebrates Rosh Hashanah"—Provided by publisher.
Identifiers: LCCN 2024038591 (print) | LCCN 2024038592 (ebook) | ISBN 9798765668764 (library binding) | ISBN 9798765684450 (paperback) | ISBN 9798765678770 (epub)
Subjects: LCSH: Rosh ha-Shanah—Juvenile literature.
Classification: LCC BM695.N5 P48 2026 (print) | LCC BM695.N5 (ebook) | DDC 296.4/315—dc23/eng/20241106

LC record available at https://lccn.loc.gov/2024038591
LC ebook record available at https://lccn.loc.gov/2024038592

Manufactured in the United States of America
1 – CG – 7/15/25

# Table of Contents

Celebrating Rosh Hashanah .............4

Did You See It? ........16

Index ....................16

# Celebrating Rosh Hashanah

Rosh Hashanah is
the Jewish New Year.
It happens in the fall.

We light candles. They are warm and bright.

We do good things
for others.

We eat a special meal.

We pray together.

We blow the ram's horn
to welcome the new year.

## Did You See It?

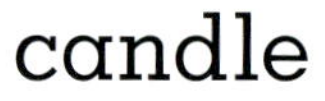

candle

meal

pray

## Index

candles, 7

fall, 5

meal, 11

new year, 5, 15

pray, 13

ram's horn, 15